Fadumo Goes Shopping

The New East Enders Series

Written by Marta Paluch

Illustrated by Mary Pierce

Gate
HOUSE

Fadumo Goes Shopping
Text copyright © Marta Paluch 2014
Illustrations copyright © Mary Pierce 2014

Published in 2014 by Gatehouse Media Limited

ISBN: 978-1-84231-088-5

British Library Cataloguing-in-Publication Data:
A catalogue record for this book is available from the British Library

Authors' Note

In 2003 the ESOL Outreach team at Tower Hamlets College gained funding from the East London ESOL Pathfinder to produce a pack of teaching materials relevant to the context of Outreach ESOL classes. Tower Hamlets College was the lead partner for the East London ESOL Pathfinder.

The resulting pack of materials included 6 easy reading booklets for beginning ESOL learners. The reading booklets proved popular and it was suggested that we should try to get them published. We approached Avantibooks who agreed to publish them as a series entitled *The New Eastenders*, but those books are now out of print.

We are delighted that they have now been given a new lease of life by Gatehouse Books as *The New East Enders Series* for a new generation of ESOL learners. We have added a seventh title to the series, called *My Mother-in-Law*, and a useful set of tutor resources and student worksheets. We hope you enjoy using them.

Marta Paluch & Mary Pierce

On Saturday Fadumo goes shopping
with her children.

They go to the shoe shop.
Ibrahim needs new shoes.

Fadumo likes the black leather shoes.
Ibrahim doesn't like the black leather shoes.
He likes trainers.

They buy the trainers.

FASHION WORLD
CLOTHES SHOP

SALE

They go to the clothes shop.
Zahra needs a dress.

There are lots of dresses.

Fadumo likes the green checked dress.

Zahra doesn't like the checked dress.

Zahra likes the red spotted dress
but the dress is very expensive.

Fadumo likes the blue dress with flowers.

The dress isn't expensive.

Zahra likes the dress.

They buy it.

They go to the market.
Fadumo wants vegetables.

Fadumo likes spinach
but the children don't like spinach.
Fadumo likes aubergines
but the children don't like aubergines.

Ibrahim likes tomatoes
and Zahra likes cucumbers.
They like fruit.

Fadumo buys

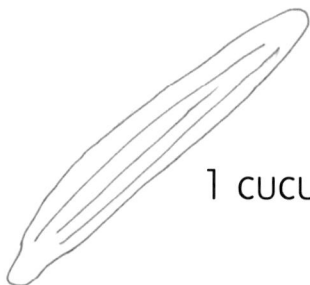

1 cucumber

Lettuces
50p each

2 lettuces

3 bunches of spinach

4 kilos of onions

5 pounds of tomatoes

6 heads of garlic

7 bananas

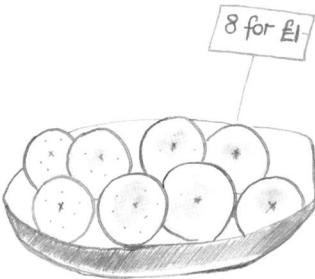

8 for £1

8 oranges

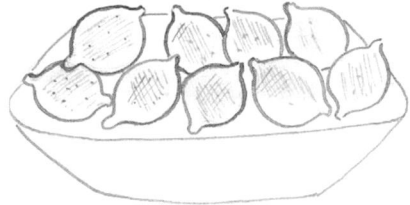

9 lemons

10lb

10 pounds of potatoes

and a big bunch of grapes.

The shopping is heavy.

Fadumo and the children are tired.

If you have enjoyed this book, why not try one of these other titles from *The New East Enders Series:*

A New Home

From Here to There

Good Neighbours

My Mother-in-Law

My Son is Sick

Rima's Day

A comprehensive set of tutor resources is available to support this series of readers:

**The New East Enders Series
Tutor Resources CD-ROM**

ISBN: 978-1-84231-094-6

Gatehouse Books®

Gatehouse Books are written for older teenagers and adults who are developing their basic reading and writing or English language skills.

The format of our books is clear and uncluttered.
The language is familiar and the text is often line-broken, so that each line ends at a natural pause.

Gatehouse Books are widely used within Adult Basic Education throughout the English speaking world. They are also a valuable resource within the Prison Education Service and Probation Services, Social Services and secondary schools - both in basic skills and ESOL teaching.

Catalogue available

Gatehouse Media Limited
PO Box 965
Warrington
WA4 9DE

Tel/Fax: 01925 267778
E-mail: info@gatehousebooks.com
Website: www.gatehousebooks.com